RYA VHF R

Short Range Certificate
Syllabus & Sample Exam Questions

© **RYA**
Third Edition 2012
Reprinted June 2013
Reprinted December 2015, February 2017

The Royal Yachting Association
RYA House, Ensign Way,
Hamble, Southampton,
Hampshire SO31 4YA

Tel: 02380 604 100
E-mail: publications@rya.org.uk
Web: www.rya.org.uk
Follow us on Twitter @RYAPublications or on YouTube

ISBN 9781906435851
RYA Order Code: G26

Note: While all reasonable care has been taken in the preparation of this
book, the publisher takes no responsibility for the use of the methods or
products or contracts described in the book.

Cover design & typesetting: Jude Williams
Technical Editor: Alison Noice
Proofreading: Alan Thatcher
Printed in China through World Print
Photographs: Standard Horizon

CONTENTS

The Short Range Certificate (SRC) is the radio operator qualification which authorises the holder to operate a VHF radiotelephone, fitted with Digital Selective Calling (DSC), on board any British vessel which is voluntarily fitted with radio equipment.

The syllabus for the SRC was designed by the Conference of European Posts and Telecommunications (CEPT) as a standard qualification for the operation of equipment using procedures and techniques of the Global Maritime Distress and Safety System (GMDSS).

If you do not hold a certificate there are two ways to obtain the SRC. It can be awarded either on satisfactory completion of an assessed course carried out at an **RYA** Recognised Training Centre or by taking an examination.

Courses and examinations cover all aspects of marine band VHF radio communication. Shorter courses and examinations are available for candidates who hold non-GMDSS radio operator certificates and who wish to convert to a GMDSS qualification.

Restricted (VHF only) Radio Operator Certificates of Competence issued prior to 1 September 2000 remain valid qualifications for the operation of non-GMDSS VHF radiotelephones.

To be able to answer the test questions in this book you will need to read the book **G22 RYA VHF Radio** (inc. GMDSS) and/or **G31 RYA VHF Handbook.**

THE SHORT RANGE CERTIFICATE AWARD SYSTEM

The following arrangements apply to the award of the SRC. Certificates issued prior to the introduction of the SRC will continue to be valid for use with non-GMDSS equipment.

Courses

The required learning time is now 10 hours, which can include up to 3 hours' guided self-learning prior to the course. A student pack is provided by the **RYA** Recognised Training Centre, containing the **RYA** VHF Handbook and a certificate application form. The **RYA** SRC course is available as online or classroom training.

Eligibility

Candidates for SRC exams must have completed either the classroom training course or the **RYA** online course, and provide proof of completion to the examiner. Candidates are exempt from the training course if they hold a restricted VHF certificate. Proof must be provided with the certificate application form.

The Form of the Assessment

Practical assessment: Each candidate must have a dedicated training radio during their practical assessment, and a maximum of 4 candidates may be examined at any one time. The examiner will provide procedural cards or scenarios for the students.

Theory assessment paper: The written paper has a time limit of 30 minutes. Additional time may be allowed for those who have reading problems such as dyslexia. The MCA guidance is to allow an additional 8 minutes for this length of exam. The written exam is a 'closed book' exam. The examiner is responsible for ensuring there are exam papers for each candidate. Each written paper must have the examiner's assessor number added to it and be stored at the exam centre (i.e. training centre) until the next **RYA** inspection. Exam papers must be destroyed once they are no longer required. The pass mark is marked on each exam paper.

The Syllabus

The syllabus is set by the European Conference of Postal and Telecommunications Administrations (CEPT) and full details are given in Annex A (see page 17).

Application Forms and Supporting Documents

Assessment/examination application forms are provided by your **RYA** Recognised Training Centre. All applicants MUST provide a passport-size photograph of themselves when they return the application form.

Age Limit

There is no age limit for attending the course. The minimum age for sitting the examination is 16.

Quality Monitoring

Training centres are inspected by MCA/**RYA** Inspectors at regular intervals.

Examination Syllabus

The examination should consist of theoretical and practical tests and include at least:

A General knowledge of radio communications in the maritime mobile service

A.1 The general principles and basic features of the maritime mobile service.

B Detailed practical knowledge and ability to use radio equipment

B.1 The VHF radio installation. Use of VHF equipment in practice.

B.2 Purpose and use of digital selective calling features and techniques.

C Operational procedures of the GMDSS and detailed practical operation of the GMDSS subsystems and equipment

C.1 Basic introduction to GMDSS procedures.

C.2 Distress, urgency and safety communication procedures in the GMDSS.

C.3 Distress, urgency and safety communication procedures by radiotelephony in the old distress and safety system.

C.4 Protection of distress frequencies.

C.5 Maritime safety information (MSI) systems in the GMDSS.

C.6 Alerting and locating signals in the GMDSS.

D Operational procedures and regulations for radiotelephone communications

D.1 Ability to exchange communications relevant to the safety of life at sea.

D.2 Regulations, obligatory procedures and practices.

D.3 Practical and theoretical knowledge of radiotelephone procedures.

D.4 Use of the International Phonetic Alphabet and, where appropriate, parts of the IMO Standard Marine Communication Phrases.

CONTENT OF ASSESSMENT

Assessment of Practical Ability

The student can perform the following functions:

A Distress Situations

1 Define a distress situation.
2 Initiate a DSC distress alert, with position and time input manually or automatically.
3 Send a Mayday message by voice.
4 Respond appropriately to a DSC distress alert and to a Mayday message, including relay of a distress message.
5 Know how to deploy an EPIRB and a SART.
6 Know the procedure for cancellation of a distress message sent in error.

B Urgency Situations

1 Identify a situation in which an urgency message is appropriate.
2 Initiate a DSC urgency alert.
3 Send a Pan Pan message by voice.
4 Respond appropriately to an urgency message.

C Safety Situations

1 Identify a situation in which a safety message is appropriate.
2 Initiate a DSC safety alert.
3 Send a safety message by voice.
4 Receive Maritime Safety Information by NAVTEX.

D Routine Communication

1 Initiate a DSC routine call.
2 Establish communication and exchange messages with other stations by voice using appropriate channels.
3 Test the radiotelephone by means of an appropriate test call.
4 Enter a DSC group and individual MMSI.
5 Maintain an appropriate listening watch on DSC and voice channels.
6 Use the International Phonetic Alphabet.

WRITTEN TEST QUESTIONS

The written test consists of **16 questions**.

Time allowed = **30 minutes**

Part A – Distress, Urgency and Safety Procedures.
Maximum possible marks = 12. Pass mark = 9.

Part B – General questions.
Maximum possible marks = 13. Pass mark = 7.

Written test papers will be formulated from the following bank of questions.

Question 1 (3 marks)

a) *What type of DSC Alert would you send in each of the following situations? Distress, Urgency or Safety?*

1) You sight large pieces of timber floating close to the coast. There are numerous small craft in the area.

2) Engine failure in a motor cruiser being blown towards a rocky shore.

3) You sight a major explosion in a craft anchored close to your position.

b) *You receive a DSC Distress Alert and it is acknowledged by HM Coastguard. Which of the following actions would you take? Choose 3 you consider to be appropriate.*

1) Plot the casualty's position.

2) Chat to the casualty to cheer him up.

3) Send an urgency alert to 'All Ships'.

4) Keep radio silence if you cannot help.

5) Stand by to offer help to Coastguard.

6) Broadcast a Mayday Relay.

c) *What type of DSC Alert would be sent in each of the following situations? Distress, Urgency or Safety?*

1) Total engine failure in a motor cruiser drifting towards a rocky shore.

2) When the coastguard is about to announce a serious navigational hazard.

3) You sight a major explosion in a craft about a mile from you.

d) *Would you send a DSC Distress Alert in each of these situations? In each case state Yes or No.*

1) You sight a series of red parachute flares far out to sea.

2) A crew member has a serious head injury and is bleeding from the ears.

3) You notice that a large navigational buoy is adrift in a strong tidal stream.

e) *For which of the following would it be WRONG to send a DSC Distress Alert?*

1) A man has fallen overboard at night.

2) A crew member has a dislocated shoulder and is in considerable pain.

3) A motor cruiser has an engine failure in heavy weather close to a rocky lee shore.

Question 2 (2 marks)

a) *You have accidentally sent a DSC Distress Alert. Which of the following actions would you take? Choose ONE only.*

    1) Turn the set off for five minutes then switch it on again. No further action required.

    2) Turn the set off and on again, then send a DSC Urgency Alert.
Call the Coastguard to apologise.

    3) Turn the set off and on again. Call 'All Ships' on Channel 16 to cancel the distress, giving your MMSI.

    4) Leave the set switched on. Make a routine DSC call to the Coastguard to cancel the distress.

b) *You receive a DSC Distress Alert which is not acknowledged by the Coastguard. What action should you take? Choose ONE only.*

    1) Wait for the repeat alert. If there is still no acknowledgment, send a Distress Alert and Mayday Relay.

    2) Send an Urgency Alert as soon as possible then relay the Mayday message.

    3) Wait for five minutes. If there is still no acknowledgment, send an Urgency Alert and Mayday Relay.

    4) Wait for another vessel to respond with a Mayday Relay message.

c) *Give TWO circumstances when you would send a DSC Urgency Alert.*

d) *A light aircraft crashes into the sea near your boat, which is equipped with a Class D DSC VHF radio. Which ONE of the following actions will you take?*

    1) Send a DSC Distress Alert and a Mayday Relay voice message.

    2) Send a DSC Urgency Alert and a Pan Pan voice message.

    3) Send a DSC Urgency Alert and a Mayday Relay voice message.

    4) Send a DSC Mayday Relay Alert and a Mayday Relay voice message.

Question 3 (6 marks)

a) *You are alone on your motor cruiser 'Nogo'. The engine has broken down and the craft is dragging her anchor towards a rocky shore. Your position is 50° 17'.80N 004° 14'. 60W. The MMSI is 235899981 and the call sign is MZZB. Write the distress call and message you would send by voice after sending a distress alert.*

b) *Your yacht 'Wetfoot' has hit a submerged object and is sinking. With you are three friends. Your position is 50° 24'.80N 003° 04'.40W. The call-sign is 2MGM. The MMSI is 235899980. Write the distress call and message you would send by voice after sending a distress alert.*

c) *A crew member of your boat 'Mudlark' has shown all the symptoms of a heart attack and is now unconscious. Including the casualty there are three persons on board. Your position is 51° 45'.80N 001° 34'.50E. The MMSI is 235899987 and your call sign is 2ATZ. Write the distress call and message you would send by voice after sending a distress alert.*

d) *Your boat 'Sinking Feeling' is leaking and sinking with four people on board. You have an inflatable dinghy. Your position is 49° 48'.20N 005° 46'.50W. The MMSI is 235899988. Your call sign is MABC. Write the distress call and message you would send by voice after sending a distress alert.*

e) *There are four of you on board your motor cruiser 'Flam' when a serious fire breaks out. The MMSI is 235899986 and the call sign is MQVB. Your position is 51° 29'.20N 001° 42'.75E. Write the distress call and message you would send by voice after sending a distress alert.*

Question 3 cont.

f)   Your boat 'Hot Spot' has a serious engine fire. There are just two of you on board and you have a life-raft. Your position is 52° 15'.20N 005° 30'.00W. The MMSI is 235899991. Your call sign is MZCD. Write the distress call and message you would send by voice after sending a distress alert.

Question 4 (1 mark)

a)   What is the meaning of the procedure words SEELONCE MAYDAY?

b)   What is the meaning of the procedure words SEELONCE FEENEE?

c)   What procedure word is the Coastguard likely to use before announcing a new gale warning?

d)   What procedure word should be used at the beginning of every voice message concerning a distress situation?

e)   When will the Coastguard use the words 'PAN PAN'?

1) During DISTRESS working
OR
2) During URGENCY working.

Question 5 (1 mark)

a)   A Securité MESSAGE from the Coastguard is sent:

1) By voice on Channel 16 after an 'All Ships' DSC Urgency alert?

2) By voice on Channel 70 after a DSC Safety alert?

3) By voice on Channel M?

4) By voice on a working channel after a DSC Safety alert?

b)   Which one of these channels should be used to transmit an URGENCY message by voice?

1) Channel 70.

2) Channel 16.

3) Channel 03.

c)   Will a DSC All Ships Securité Alert be sent for:

1) Routine weather forecasts?

2) A new gale warning?

3) A routine individual DSC call from the Coastguard?

d)   Which of the following channels is used for club safety boats?

1) Channel 70.

2) Channel 16.

3) Channel M.

4) Channel 86.

e)   Which of the following channels is used to send a DSC All Ships Alert?

1) Channel 70.

2) Channel 16.

3) Channel 10.

4) Channel 67.

Question 6 (1 mark)

a)   *Would you expect to receive a DIGITAL acknowledgment from the Coastguard after you have sent an Urgency alert?*

Yes / No

b)   *In the UK, Channel 67 is used:*

1) By patrolling Police boats?

2) By HM Coastguard for small craft safety traffic?

3) For sending digital alerts?

4) For requesting a marina berth?

c)   *Which channel is designated as the UK small craft safety channel?*

1) Channel 6.

2) Channel 13.

3) Channel 67.

4) Channel 77.

d)   *Channel 13 is designated for:*

1) Bridge to bridge communication about the safety of navigation?

2) Ships engaged in underwater operations?

3) Communication between ships and SAR helicopters?

e)   *Which channel is allocated for Bridge to Bridge communication on matters of navigational safety?*

1) Channel 77.

2) Channel 13.

3) Channel 21.

4) Channel 80.

Question 7 (1 mark)

a)   *Which one of the following identifies the MMSI of a coast station?*

1) 002320014

2) 234678546

3) 023376543

4) 000234120

b)   *Which of the following characteristics identify the MMSI of a group call?*

1) Commences with three-digit country MID.

2) Commences with a single zero.

3) Commences with two zeros.

4) Ends with two zeros.

Question 7 cont.

c) *Which of the following identifies a Group MMSI?*

  1) 002320014
  2) 023376543
  3) 234678546
  4) 000234120

d) *Why is it impossible to hear another boat calling a UK marina when using a Class D VHF radio on Channel 80?*

  1) Marinas cannot talk to two boats.
  2) Because Channel 80 is a duplex channel.
  3) Class D sets cannot use Channel 80.
  4) Because Channel 80 is a simplex channel.

Question 8 (1 mark)

a) *When making initial contact, should the name of the boat you are calling be repeated:*

  1) Once?
  2) Three times?
  3) Any number between one and three times depending on the circumstances?

b) *You wish to contact a boat but don't know its MMSI. Should you:*

  1) Make a DSC All Ships call?
  2) Call the boat by name on Channel 16?
  3) Call the boat by name on Channel 70?
  4) Make a DSC routine call but without inserting the MMSI?

c) *You speak to your nearest Coastguard who has a 100m aerial. Your aerial is 16m high and you are using high power. What is the greatest distance you could be from his aerial in normal conditions?*

  1) 4–5 nautical miles.
  2) 10–20 nautical miles.
  3) 30–45 nautical miles.
  4) 400–500 nautical miles.

d) *Vessels using DSC are identified by:*

  1) Their MMSI?
  2) Their international call-sign?
  3) Their HIN?
  4) The name and, if necessary to avoid ambiguity, their base port'?

Question 9 (2 marks)

a) *Give the phonetic words for the following letters:*

    E   H   Z   Y   I   W

b) *Give the phonetic words for the following letters:*

    A   D   L   N   P   S

c) *Give the phonetic words for the following letters:*

    C   F   J   L   U   V

d) *Give the phonetic words for the following letters:*

    B   E   M   O   R   T

e) *Give the phonetic words for the following letters:*

    B   X   S   G   K   Q

f) *Give the phonetic words for the following letters:*

    A   F   J   P   T   W

Question 10 (1 mark)

a) *Is the maximum permitted radiated power of a ship's marine band VHF radiotelephone:*

1) 25 watts?

2) 40 watts?

3) 1 watt?

b) *Should the power used for routine transmissions be:*

1) The maximum power in order to ensure good communication?

2) The minimum power which will allow communication between the stations involved?

3) Low power in order to conserve the boat's battery?

c) *You wish to make a radio check. Would you:*

1) Call 'All Ships' on Channel 16 and ask for a radio check?

2) Call another boat or a marina?

3) Call the Coastguard on your mobile?

4) Send a DSC Safety Alert and ask for a radio check?

d) *Is the purpose of the low power switch:*

1) To conserve the vessel's battery?

2) To avoid disturbance by reducing the volume?

3) To limit the range of the transmission when speaking to another station at close range?

4) To dim the illumination on the display?

Question 11 (1 mark)

a) *A call to a Harbour Control Centre should be made on which channel?*
   1) Channel 6.
   2) Channel 16.
   3) Channel 72.
   4) The port operations channel.

b) *Which one of these channels should NOT be used for inter-ship working?*
   1) Channel 70.
   2) Channel 72.
   3) Channel 08.
   4) Channel 77.

c) *Channel M should be used for which of the following?*
   1) Digital distress alerting.
   2) Club safety boats.
   3) Port operations.
   4) Broadcasting tidal information.

d) *When making initial contact with another ship not fitted with DSC should you call:*
   1) By voice on Channel 70?
   2) On Channel M?
   3) On Channel 16 and suggest an inter-ship channel?
   4) Direct on Channel 72 and hope he will be on that channel?

Question 12 (1 mark)

a) *Does NAVTEX offer a system for:*
   1) The correction of electronic charts?
   2) Texting your position to other vessels?
   3) Receiving gale warnings and navigational warnings at sea?
   4) Plotting the vessel's ground track?

b) *NAVTEX is:*
   1) A chart plotting instrument?
   2) A system for receiving gale and navigational warnings?
   3) A radar alerting system?
   4) A port control system?

c) *The NAVTEX service can be used:*
   1) To request weather and navigational information from the Coastguard?
   2) To receive weather, navigational and safety information on a vessel at sea?
   3) To text the Coastguard?
   4) To send weather reports to the Met Office?

Question 12 cont.

d) *Which electronic navigational aid can be interfaced with a DSC controller to input position?*

1) NAVTEX.

2) GPS.

3) Fluxgate compass and electronic log.

4) Radar.

e) *Does a SART:*

a) Send a coded signal to a search and rescue satellite?

b) Alert the closest Search & Rescue centre as soon as it is deployed?

c) Display a series of dots on the radar screens of vessels within range?

Question 13 (1 mark)

a) *With whom should you register your EPIRB?*

1) The manufacturer.

2) The owner's shore-side contact.

3) The national EPIRB registry.

4) The RNLI.

b) *Does a SART:*

1) Send a coded signal to a Search & Rescue satellite?

2) Alert the closest rescue centre as soon as it is deployed?

3) Display a seies of dots on the radar screens of vessels within range?

c) *If you inadvertently activate an EPIRB, should you:*

1) Throw it overboard in a weighted sack?

2) Switch it off as soon as possible?

3) Call the Coastguard to tell them that you have activated the beacon?

4) Wrap the aerial in tin foil to stop the signal from radiating?

d) *SART stands for:*

1) Simplex aerial for Radio Telephony?

2) Search and Rescue Transceiver?

3) Search areas for Rescue Transports?

4) Search and Rescue Transponder?

Question 14 (1 mark)

a) *Is it permissible to hold a discussion on the fortunes of a football team with another vessel on an inter-ship channel?*

   1) Yes.

   2) No.

b) *Which one of the following is permitted according to the Radio Regulations?*

   1) Sending a routine DSC Alert to another ship station.

   2) Sending an Urgency Alert to test DSC.

   3) Whistling into the microphone to attract attention.

c) *Which one of following calls is permitted?*

   1) A test call by voice on Channel 80.

   2) A call without identity.

   3) A test call by voice on Channel 70.

   4) A hoax distress call.

d) *Which one of the following is permitted?*

   1) A call containing music.

   2) A call addressed to an unofficial shore station.

   3) A call to another vessel on Channel 72.

   4) An unsupervised call by a 14 year old.

e) *Which one of following calls is allowed?*

   1) A call containing indecent language.

   2) A call addressed to a friend at home with a hand-held VHF radio.

   3) A call to marina on Channel 80.

   4) A call on Channel 67 to another vessel about a party.

Question 15 (1 mark)

a) *Which of the following procedure words would be correct at the termination of working?*

   1) Over.

   2) Over and out.

   3) Out.

   4) Logging off.

b) *In the UK, call-signs and MMSIs are allocated by:*

   1) Ofcom?

   2) The MCA?

   3) The **RYA**?

   4) Harbour Masters?

Question 15 cont.

c) *How would you end a transmission for which you expect a reply?*

1) Out.

2) Over and out.

3) Come in.

4) Over.

d) *You call another boat by voice but receive no response. How long should you wait before calling again?*

1) Call immediately.

2) Call after 1 minute.

3) Call after 2 minutes.

4) Call after 3 minutes.

Question 16 (1 mark)

a) *Who is the issuing authority for Ship Radio Licences in the UK?*

1) The **RYA**.

2) The Home Office.

3) Ofcom.

4) British Telecom.

b) *Can a hand-held radio be used in the tender under the authority of the parent vessel's Ship Radio Licence?*

1) Yes.

2) No.

c) *Is it legal to use a portable VHF to call your boat from the chandlery in the marina?*

1) Yes.

2) No.

d) *Which one of the following does not have to be included on an application form for a Ship Radio Licence?*

1) Naxtex.

2) Radar.

3) Handheld VHF radio.

4) EPIRB.

e) *You purchase a handheld radio to take with you on a charter boat. What type of licence, if any, does it require?*

1) Ship Radio Licence.

2) Leisure Boater's Licence.

3) Ship Portable Radio Licence.

4) Does not require a licence.

FULL SYLLABUS FOR THE CEPT SHORT RANGE CERTIFICATE

A The general principles and basic features of the maritime mobile service relevant to vessels NOT subject to a compulsory fit under the SOLAS convention.

1.1 Types of communication of the maritime mobile service.
Distress, urgency and safety communications.
Public correspondence.
Port operations service.
Ship movement service.
Intership communication.
On board communications.

1.2 Types of station in the maritime mobile service.
Ship stations.
Coast stations.
Pilot stations, port stations etc.
Aircraft stations.
Rescue Co-ordination Centres (RCC).

1.3 Elementary knowledge of radio frequencies and channels appropriate to the VHF maritime mobile band.
The concept of frequency.
Propagation on VHF frequencies.
Range for voice communications.
Range for DSC transmissions.
The usage of VHF frequencies in the maritime mobile service.
The concept of radio channel: simplex, semi-duplex and duplex.
Channel plan for VHF, including allocations for the GMDSS.
Distress and safety channels.
National channels for small craft safety.
Intership communications.
Port operations.
Ship movement.
Calling channels.
Public correspondence channels.

1.4 Functionality of ship station equipment.
Sources of energy of ship stations.
Batteries: types and characteristics, charging, maintenance.

ANNEX A

B Detailed working knowledge of radio equipment.

B1 The VHF radio installation.
  1.1 Radiotelephone channels.
      Channel selection and controls.
      Dual watch facilities and controls.
  1.2 Basic controls and usage, e.g.:
      Connecting and power.
      Press to transmit switch.
      High/low output power switch.
      Volume control.
      Squelch control.
      Dimmer.
  1.3 Portable two-way VHF radiotelephone apparatus.
  1.4 Maritime VHF antennas.

B2 Purpose and use of Digital Selective Calling (DSC) facilities.
  2.1 The general principles and basic features of DSC.
      DSC messages.
      DSC attempt.
      Call acknowledgement.
      Call relay.
  2.2 Types of call:
      Distress call.
      All ships call.
      Call to individual station.
      Geographical area call.
      Group call.
  2.3 The Maritime Mobile Service Identity (MMSI) number system.
      Nationality identification: Maritime Identification Digits (MID)
      Ship station numbers.
      Coast station numbers.
  2.4 Call categorisation and priority.
      Distress.
      Urgency.
      Safety.
      Ship's business.
      Routine.

2.5 Call telecommand and traffic information.

Distress alerts.

Other calls.

Working channel information.

2.6 VHF DSC facilities and usage.

Channel 70 instant alert selector.

DSC data entry and display.

Updating vessel position.

Entering pre-set message.

Entering traffic information.

Reviewing received messages.

DSC watchkeeping functions and controls.

C Operational procedures of the GMDSS and detailed practical operation of GMDSS subsystems and equipment.

C1 Search and Rescue (SAR) Procedures in the Global Maritime Distress and Safety System (GMDSS).

1.1 Sea Areas and access to GMDSS facilities.

1.2 The role of RCCs.

1.3 Organisation of search and rescue.

C2 Distress, urgency and safety communication procedures in the GMDSS.

2.1 Distress communications via VHF DSC equipment.

DSC distress alert.

The definition of a distress alert.

Transmission of a distress alert.

Transmission of a shore-to-ship distress alert relay.

Transmission of a distress alert by a station not itself in distress.

Receipt and acknowledgement of VHF DSC distress alert.

Acknowledgement procedure.

Receipt and acknowledgement by a coast station.

Receipt and acknowledgement by a ship station.

Handling of distress alerts.

Preparations for handling of distress traffic.

Distress traffic terminology.

On-scene communications.

SAR operation.

2.2 Urgency and Safety communications via DSC equipment.
The meaning of urgency and safety communications.
Procedures for DSC urgency and safety calls.
Urgency communications.
Safety communications.

C3 Protection of distress frequencies.

3.1 Avoiding harmful interference.
Avoiding the transmission of false alerts.
Status of Channel 70.
3.2 Transmission during distress traffic.
3.3 Prevention of unauthorised transmissions.
3.4 Test protocols and procedures.
Testing DSC equipment.
Radiotelephone test procedures.
3.5 Avoidance of transmissions in VHF guard bands.
3.6 Procedures to follow when a false distress alert is transmitted.

C4 Maritime Safety Information.

4.1 The NAVTEX system.
Purpose and capabilities, including distress and safety functions.

C5 Alerting and Locating Signals.

5.1 Purpose and definition.
5.2 Emergency Position Indication Radio Beacons (EPIRBs).
Registration and coding.
Operation, including automatic and manual activation.
COSPAS/SARSAT 406 MHz EPIRB.
Inmarsat-E 1.6 GHz EPIRB.
VHF-DSC EPIRB.
121.5MHz homing function.
Mounting considerations.
Routine maintenance.
Testing.
Checking battery expiry date.
Checking the float-free mechanism.
5.3 Search and Rescue Transponder (SART).
Operation.
Operating height.
Effect of radar reflector.
Range of an SART transmitter.

D   Operational procedures and regulations for VHF radiotelephone communications.

D1   Ability to exchange communications relevant to the safety of life at sea.

1.1   Distress communications.

Distress signal.

The correct use and meaning of the signal MAYDAY.

Distress call.

Distress message.

Acknowledgement of a distress message.

Obligation to acknowledge a distress message.

Correct form of acknowledgement.

Action to be taken following acknowledgement.

The control of distress traffic.

The correct use and meanings of the signals.

SEELONCE MAYDAY.

SEELONCE FEENEE.

Transmission of a distress message by a station not itself in distress.

The correct use and meaning of the signal MAYDAY RELAY.

1.2   Urgency communications.

Urgency signal.

The correct use and meaning of the signal PAN-PAN.

Urgency message: obtaining urgent medical advice through a coast station.

1.3   Safety communications.

Safety signal: the correct use and meaning of the signal SECURITÉ.

Safety message.

Special procedures for communication with appropriate national organisations on matters affecting safety.

1.4   Reception of MSI by VHF radiotelephone.

1.5   Awareness of the existence and use of the IMO Standard Marine Navigational Vocabulary.

Knowledge of the following basic signals:

ALL AFTER; ALL BEFORE;

CORRECT; CORRECTION;

I SAY AGAIN; I SPELL;

IN FIGURES; IN LETTERS;

OUT; OVER; RADIO CHECK;

READ BACK; RECEIVED;

SAY AGAIN; STATION CALLING;

TEXT; THIS IS; TRAFFIC; WAIT;

WORD AFTER; WORD BEFORE;

WRONG.

1.6   Use of the International Phonetic Alphabet.

D2 Regulations. Obligatory procedures and practices.

2.1 Awareness of international documentation and availability of national publications.

2.2 Knowledge of the international regulations and agreements governing the maritime mobile service.

Requirement for Ship Station Licence.

Regulations concerning control of the operation of radio equipment by the holder of an appropriate certificate of competence.

National regulations concerning radio record keeping.

Preservation of the secrecy of correspondence.

Types of call and types of message which are prohibited.

D3 Practical and theoretical knowledge of radiotelephone call procedures.

3.1 Method of calling a Coast Station by radiotelephony.

Ordering a manually switched link-call.

Ending the call.

Calls to ships from Coast Stations.

Special facilities of calls.

Method of calling a Coast Station DSC for general communications.

Electing an automatic radiotelephone call.

3.2 Traffic charges.

International charging system.

Accounting Authority Identification Code (AAIC).

3.3 Practical traffic routines.

Correct use of call signs.

Procedure for establishing communication on:

intership, public correspondence, small craft safety, port operations and ship movement channels.

Procedure for unanswered calls and garbled calls.

Control of communications.

EXTRACTS FROM MARINE GUIDANCE NOTE MGN 324 (M+F)

Guidance on the use of VHF Radio and Automatic Identification Systems (AIS) at Sea

Notice to all Owners, Masters, Officers and Pilots of Merchant Ships, Owners and Skippers of Fishing Vessels and Owners of Yachts and Pleasure Craft.

This notice replaces Marine Guidance Notes MGN 22, 167 & 277.

Summary

Given the continuing number of casualties where the misuse of VHF radio has been established as a contributory factor it has been decided to re-issue the MCA Operational Guidance Notes on the use of VHF Radio. It has also been decided to include operational guidance notes for AIS equipment on board ship formerly contained in Marine Guidance Note 277.

1. The International Maritime Organisation (IMO) has noted with concern the widespread misuse of VHF channels at sea especially the distress, safety and calling Channels 16 (156.8 MHz) and 70 (156.525 MHz), and channels used for port operations, ship movement services and reporting systems. Although VHF at sea makes an important contribution to navigation safety, its misuse causes serious interference and, in itself, becomes a danger to safety at sea. IMO has asked Member Governments to ensure that VHF channels are used correctly.

2. All users of marine VHF on United Kingdom vessels, and all other vessels in UK territorial waters and harbours, are therefore reminded, in conformance with international and national legislation, marine VHF apparatus may only be used in accordance with the International Telecommunications Union's (ITU) Radio Regulations.

These Regulations specifically prescribe that:

    (a) Channel 16 may only be used for distress, urgency and very brief safety communications and for calling to establish other communications which should then be concluded on a suitable working channel;

    (b) Channel 70 may only be used for Digital Selective Calling not oral communication;

    (c) On VHF channels allocated to port operations or ship movement services such as VTS, the only messages permitted are restricted to those relating to operational handling, the movement and the safety of ships and to the safety of persons;

    (d) All signals must be preceded by an identification, e.g. the vessel's name or callsign;

    (e) The service of every VHF radio telephone station must be controlled by an operator holding a certificate issued or recognised by the station's controlling administration. This is usually the country of registration, if the vessel is registered. Providing the station is so controlled, other persons besides the holder of the certificate may use the equipment.

(Paragraphs 3 & 4 omitted)

5. Channels 6, 8, 72 and 77 have been made available, in UK waters, for routine ship-to-ship communications. Masters, Skippers and Owners are urged to ensure that all ship-to-ship communications working in these waters is confined to these channels, selecting the channel most appropriate in the local conditions at the time.

6. Channel 13 is designated for use on a worldwide basis as a navigation safety communication channel, primarily for intership navigation safety communications. It may also be used for the ship movement and port services.

Use of VHF as Collision Avoidance Aid

7. There have been a significant number of collisions where subsequent investigation has found that at some stage before impact, one or both parties were using VHF radio in an attempt to avoid collision. The use of VHF radio in these circumstances is not always helpful and may even prove to be dangerous.

8. At night, in restricted visibility or when there are more than two vessels in the vicinity, the need for positive identification is essential but this can rarely be guaranteed. Uncertainties can arise over the identification of vessels and the interpretation of messages received. Even where positive identification has been achieved there is still the possibility of a misunderstanding due to language difficulties however fluent the parties concerned might be in the language being used. An imprecise or ambiguously expressed message could have serious consequences.

9. Valuable time can be wasted whilst mariners on vessels approaching each other try to make contact on VHF radio instead of complying with the Collision Regulations. There is the further danger that even if contact and identification is achieved and no difficulties over the language of communication or message content arise, a course of action might still be chosen that does not comply with the Collision Regulations. This may lead to the collision it was intended to prevent.

10. In 1995, the judge in a collision case said "It is very probable that the use of VHF radio for conversation between these ships was a contributory cause of this collision, if only because it distracted the officers on watch from paying careful attention to their radar. I must repeat, in the hope that it will achieve some publicity, what I have said on previous occasions that any attempt to use VHF to agree the manner of passing is fraught with the danger of misunderstanding. Marine Superintendents would be well advised to prohibit such use of VHF radio and to instruct their officers to comply with the Collision Regulations."

11. In a case published in 2002 one of two vessels, approaching each other in fog, used the VHF radio to call for a red to red (port to port) passing. The call was acknowledged by the other vessel but unfortunately, due to the command of English on the calling vessel, what the caller intended was a green to green (starboard to starboard) passing. The actions were not effectively monitored by either of the vessels and collision followed.

12. Again in a case published in 2006 one of two vessels, approaching one another to involve a close quarter's situation, agreed to a starboard to starboard passing arrangement with a person on board another, unidentified ship, but not the approaching vessel. Furthermore, the passing agreement required one of the vessels to make an alteration of course, contrary to the requirements of the applicable Rule in the COLREGS. Had the vessel agreed to a passing arrangement requiring her to manoeuvre in compliance with the COLREGS, the ships would have passed clear, despite the misidentification of ships on the VHF radio. Unfortunately by the time both vessels realised that the ships had turned towards each other the distance between them had further reduced to the extent that the last minute avoiding action taken by both ships was unable to prevent a collision.

13. Although the practice of using VHF radio as a collision avoidance aid may be resorted to on occasion, for example in pilotage waters, the risks described in this note should be clearly understood and the Collision Regulations complied with.

ANNEX B

APPENDIX I
Guidance on the use of VHF at sea
(Extract from: IMO Res A.954 (23). Proper use of VHF Channels at Sea (Adopted on 5th Dec 2003))

1. VHF Communication Technique

1.1 Preparation
Before transmitting, think about the subjects which have to be communicated and, if necessary, prepare written notes to avoid unnecessary interruptions and ensure that no valuable time is wasted on a busy channel.

1.2 Listening
Listen before commencing to transmit to make certain that the channel is not already in use. This will avoid unnecessary and irritating interference.

1.3 Discipline
VHF equipment should be used correctly and in accordance with the Radio Regulations. The following in particular should be avoided:

(a) calling on Channel 16 for purposes other than distress, and very brief safety communications, when another calling channel is available;

(b) non-essential transmissions, e.g. needless and superfluous signals and correspondence;

(c) communications not related to safety and navigation on port operation channels;

(d) communication on Channel 70 other than for Digital Selective Calling;

(e) occupation of one particular channel under poor conditions;

(f) transmitting without correct identification;

(g) use of offensive language.

1.4 Repetition
Repetition of words and phrases should be avoided unless specifically requested by the receiving station.

1.5 Power reduction
When possible, the lowest transmitter power necessary for satisfactory communication should be used.

1.6 Automatic Identification System (AIS)
AIS is used for the exchange of data in ship-to-ship communications and also in communication with shore facilities. The purpose of AIS is to help identify vessels, assist in target tracking, simplify information exchange and provide additional information to assist situational awareness. AIS may be used together with VHF voice communications.

AIS should be operated in accordance with Resolution A.917 (22) as amended by Resolution A.956 (23) on Guidelines for the onboard operation use of ship-borne automatic identification systems.

1.7 Communications with coast stations
(a) On VHF channels allocated to port operations service, the only messages permitted are restricted to those relating to the operational handling, the movement and safety of ships and, in emergency, to the safety of persons. The use of these channels for ship-to-ship communications may cause serious interference to communications related to the movement and safety of shipping in port areas.

(b) Instructions given on communication matters by shore stations should be obeyed. Communications should be carried out on the channel indicated by the shore station. When a change of channel is requested, this should be acknowledged by the ship.

(c) On receiving instructions from a shore station to stop transmitting, no further communications should be made until otherwise notified (the shore station may be receiving distress or safety messages and any other transmissions could cause interference).

1.8 Communications with other ships

VHF Channel 13 is designated by the Radio Regulations for bridge to bridge communications. The ship called may indicate another working channel on which further transmissions should take place. The calling ship should acknowledge acceptance before changing channels. The listening procedure outlined above should be followed before communications are commenced on the chosen channel.

1.9 Distress communications

Distress calls/messages have absolute priority over all other communications. When heard, all other transmissions should cease and a listening watch should be kept. Any distress call/message should be recorded in the ship's log and passed to the master. On receipt of a distress message, if in the vicinity, immediately acknowledge receipt. If not in the vicinity, allow a short interval of time to elapse before acknowledging receipt of the message in order to permit ships nearer to the distress to do so.

1.10 Calling

In accordance with the radio regulations Channel 16 may only be used for distress, urgency and very brief safety communications and for calling to establish other communications which should then be conducted on a suitable working channel.

Whenever possible, a working frequency should be used for calling. If a working frequency is not available, Channel 16 may be used, provided it is not occupied by a distress call/message. In case of difficulty to establish contact with a ship or shore station, allow adequate time before repeating the call. Do not occupy the channel unnecessarily and try another channel.

1.11 Changing channels

If communications on a channel are unsatisfactory, indicate change of channel and await confirmation.

1.12 Spelling

If spelling becomes necessary use the spelling table contained in the International Code of Signals and the radio regulations and the IMO Standard Marine Communication Phrases (SMCP).

1.13 Addressing

The words "I" and "You" should be used prudently. Indicate to whom they refer.

Example of good practice:

"Seaship, this is Port Radar, Port Radar, do you have a pilot?"

"Port Radar, this is Seaship, I do have a pilot."

1.14 Watchkeeping

Every ship, while at sea, is required to maintain watches. Continuous watch keeping is required on VHF DSC Channel 70 and also when practicable, a continuous listening watch on VHF Channel 16.

APPENDIX III

Operation of AIS on board

(Extract from IMO Resolution A.917. (22). Guidelines for the onboard operational use of shipborne Automatic Identification Systems (AIS) (Adopted on 29th November 2001). As amended by Resolution A.956. (23). (Adopted 5th December 2003).)

Inherent limitations of AIS

31. The officer of the watch (OOW) should always be aware that other ships, in particular leisure craft, fishing boats and warships, and some coastal shore stations including Vessel Traffic Service (VTS) centres, might not be fitted with AIS.

32. The OOW should always be aware that other ships fitted with AIS as a mandatory carriage requirement might switch off AIS under certain circumstances by professional judgement of the master.

33. In other words, the information given by the AIS may not be a complete picture of the situation around the ship.

34. The users must be aware that transmission of erroneous information implies a risk to other ships as well as their own. The users remain responsible for all information entered into the system and the information added by the sensors.

35. The accuracy of the information received is only as good as the accuracy of the AIS information transmitted.

36. The OOW should be aware that poorly configured or calibrated ship sensors (position, speed and heading sensors) might lead to incorrect information being transmitted. Incorrect information about one ship displayed on the bridge of another could be dangerously confusing.

37. If no sensor is installed or if the sensor (e.g. the gyro) fails to provide data, the AIS automatically transmits the 'not available' data value. However the built in integrity check cannot validate the contents of the data processed by the AIS.

38. It would not be prudent for the OOW to assume that the information received from the other ship is of a comparable quality and accuracy to that which might be available on own ship.

Use of AIS in collision avoidance situations

39. The potential of AIS as an anti-collision device is recognised and AIS may be recommended as such a device in due time.

40. Nevertheless, AIS information may be used to assist collision avoidance decision making. When using the AIS in the ship to ship mode for anti-collision purposes, the following precautionary points should be borne in mind:

    (a) AIS is an additional source of navigational information. It does not replace, but supports, navigational systems such as radar target tracking and VTS; and

    (b) The use of AIS does not negate the responsibility of the OOW to comply at all times with the Collision Regulations.

41. The user should not rely on AIS as the sole information system, but should make use of all safety relevant information available.

(Sections 42 to 47 omitted as currently more relevant to large ships.)

ANNEX B

More Information

Navigation Safety Branch

Maritime and Coastguard Agency Bay 2/29

Spring Place
105 Commercial Road
Southampton SO15 1EG

+44 (0) 23 8032 9146
+44 (0) 23 8032 9204

Navigationsafety@mcga.gov.uk

Published: July 2006
© Crown Copyright 2006
MCA Website Address: www.mcga.gov.uk

RYA Training Courses

for all ages, abilities and aspirations

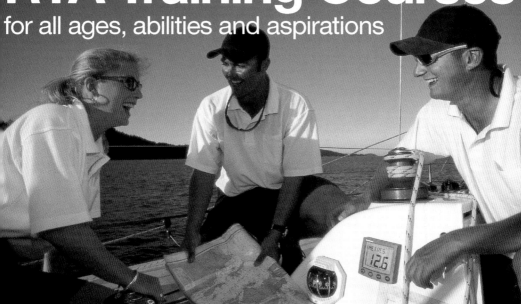

Get the most from your time on the water with our range of practical and shorebased courses.

Sail cruising from the beginners' Start Yachting course to Yachtmaster®

Motor cruising from the introductory Helmsman's course to Yachtmaster®

Sailing Away School of Sailing

Graham Snook/MBM

Also, a whole range of navigation and specialist short courses:

> **ESSENTIAL NAVIGATION AND SEAMANSHIP**

> **DAY SKIPPER**

> **COASTAL SKIPPER/ YACHTMASTER® OFFSHORE**

> **YACHTMASTER® OCEAN**

> **DIESEL ENGINE**

> **OFFSHORE SAFETY**

> **VHF RADIO**

> **RADAR**

> **SEA SURVIVAL**

> **FIRST AID**

RYA

For further information see www.rya.org.uk, call 00 44 (0)23 8060 4158 for a brochure or email training@rya.org.uk

www.rya.org.uk/go/join

LOVE YACHT CRUISING?
Then why not join the association that supports you?
Join the RYA today and benefit from

- Representing your interests and defending your rights of navigation
- Your International Certificate of Competence at no charge
- World leading Yachtmaster™ scheme
- Free sail numbers for Gold Members
- Personal advice and information on a wide range of cruising topics
- Legal advice on buying and selling a boat and other boating related matters
- The latest news delivered to your door or inbox by RYA magazine and e-newsletters
- Boat show privileges including an exclusive free RYA members' lounge
- Discounts on a wide range of products and services including boat insurance

Get more from your boating; support the RYA

Want to know more?

Then call our friendly and helpful membership team on 02380 604 100 or email: member.services@rya.org.uk

The RYA... be part of it   www.rya.org.uk

Shop online at
www.rya.org.uk/shop